MW01598727

VEGAN CANDY

© Copyright 2019 by Polly Martin All rights reserved.

This document is geared towards providing exact and reliable information in regards to the topic and issue covered. The publication is sold with the idea that the publisher is not required to render accounting, officially permitted, or otherwise, qualified services. If advice is necessary, legal or professional, a practiced individual in the profession should be ordered.

- From a Declaration of Principles which was accepted and approved equally by a Committee of the American Bar Association and a Committee of Publishers and Associations.

In no way is it legal to reproduce, duplicate, or transmit any part of this document in either electronic means or in printed format. Recording of this publication is strictly prohibited and any storage of this document is not allowed unless with written permission from the publisher. All rights reserved.

The information provided herein is stated to be truthful and consistent, in that any liability, in terms of inattention or otherwise, by any usage or abuse of any policies, processes, or directions contained within is the solitary and utter responsibility of the recipient reader. Under no circumstances will any legal responsibility or blame be held against the publisher for any reparation, damages, or monetary loss due to the information herein, either directly or indirectly.

Respective authors own all copyrights not held by the publisher.

The information herein is offered for informational purposes solely, and is universal as so. The presentation of the information is without contract or any type of guarantee assurance.

TABLE OF CONTENTS

INTRODUCTION

Filled with an abundance of sweet and easy recipes, our book Vegan Candy will encourage people of any age to make their own candy at home. The cookbook contains a collection of vegan candies to try. The recipes inside are listed with their complete ingredients, directions that are easy to follow, and their nutritional facts per serving.

With a wide array of both hard candy and gummies, you'll be able to expand your vegan diet. Though some treats may be time consuming to make, they are nonetheless simple. By following these vegan-friendly recipes, you'll be able to experience the fun of making as well as sharing deliciously sweet candies.

You will also receive a brief background to veganism. Readers will be able to learn more about the lifestyle, as well as the benefits that come from it.

The book will also be able to define popular candy making terms, brief descriptions of needed equipment, and various vegan alternatives you can use to make other dishes.

This cookbook aims to break the barriers of candy making by introducing a vegan twist. It is crafted to educate individuals and influence healthier food options, while still being able to satisfy your sweet tooth. If you are a fellow vegan, you can use this as a way to introduce your diet to others.

CHAPTER 1:

INTRODUCTION TO VEGANISM

You may have noticed that almost every popular dish seems to have a vegan alternative. Since the 2010's, veganism has become widely acknowledged and seems to keep rising in popularity. As one of the lifestyles many people live by, veganism encourages people to avoid any food that contains animal by-products. Their diet consists of plant based foods.

Not all people choose to fully commit to veganism. People known as flexitarians are known to consume animal by-products occasionally. However, they opt for plant based foods a majority of the time.

Benefits of Being a Vegan

There are various reasons why people choose to convert to veganism. Some people choose to be vegan to live a healthier lifestyle. Others use veganism as a way of saving the environment. Animal rights activists take their pledge to be a vegan as a stand against the slaughtering of animals. Lastly, people choose to be vegan in order to conserve the planet's food supply.

Good for Health

Over consumption of animal by-products can lead to serious health conditions such as cancer, heart disease, and obesity.

Anti - Cancer

Dairy can be a contributing factor to cancer development. According to Health Line, excessive consumption of dairy products is positively linked to prostate cancer. Although dairy does have its benefits, the United States Department of Agriculture (USDA).

Prevents Diabetes

Not only do plant based foods prevent cancer, but they also protect the body against obesity and Type 2 Diabetes. Although there are no direct cures to combat against obesity, veganism can definitely provide healthier food options for overweight people. In fact, several studies prove that vegans are physically lean, have less amounts of body fat, and possess lower body mass index (BMI).

Decreases Risk of Cardiovascular Diseases

Aside from cancer and obesity, following a vegan diet protects your body from developing heart disease. Just eating red meat alone can increase the risk of cardiovascular diseases by 1000 percent. On the other hand, converting to a vegan diet can lessen chances by 40 percent. It can also decrease hypertension by 34 percent, coronary heart disease by 40 percent, and unclog arteries.

Good for the Environment

In addition to the its health benefits, veganism is great for the environment.

Saves Clean Water

One of the things some humans take for granted is having access to clean water. Negative factors such as climate change, pollution, and excessive usage limit the Earth's supply.

It takes a lot of fresh water consumption in order to raise livestock. They also are the cause of frequent pollution in fresh water reserves. Reports have shown that it takes about 100 - 200 times more water to make a lb beef compared to a lb plant based food.

Good for Soil

Livestock also are known to deteriorate soil. Because having livestock includes having sufficient space to raise them, it could also lead to further deforestation.

Lessens Energy Consumption

The procedure of turning livestock into a meal requires enormous energy consumption. The mere amount of energy it takes to feed them could be used in more efficient ways. After obtaining the meat or other by-products, they must be refrigerated and transported to local markets.

Cleaner Air

Plants are known to purify the air. Research shows that livestock can cause more air pollution than all modes of transportation combined.

Protects Animal Rights

Many animal activists groups such as People for the Ethical Treatment of Animals (PETA) and Human Society of the United States (HSUS) often encourage others to become vegan or vegetarian because they view the slaughtering of animals to be unfair.

Not only are livestock commonly raised in low quality environments, but they are often shoved and compressed into a truck. They have to endure the trip from farm to slaughterhouse. The drive could take long hours or even days to reach the destination, which includes no access to basic needs such as food, water, and rest.

The livestock are either too weak, injured, or sick when they have reached the slaughterhouse. They are to be dragged off in ropes or chains. Some animals are lucky enough to survive the trip, but are frightened upon arrival. They are shocked, dragged off in chains, or even beaten when they don't comply.

Conserve Food Supply

With over seven billion people (and counting) in the world, it seems that consuming a sufficient amount of food has become a worldwide problem. Because of the imbalance between the demand for food and the ever increasing population, it seems appropriate for people to opt for more sustainable foods.

Not only do plant based foods use less resources, but it can also feed more people.

Veganism is a Win-Win Situation

Whether you choose to follow a vegan diet or stick to omnivorous ways, vegan food can be enjoyed by everyone. Though veganism requires restraining yourself from meat and by-products, there are several alternatives that you can incorporate into any dish.

CHAPTER 2:

HOW CANDY IS MADE AND THE TOOLS YOU'LL NEED

Now that you understand the various benefits that come with veganism, let's move onto what you may need in order to proceed with the following recipes.

Making vegan candy is practically the same process as making regular candy, just with healthier and more organic results. Though veganism requires restraining yourself from meat and by-products, there are an abundance of vegan alternatives that you can incorporate when making any kind of food.

While making these recipes, you will come across the following terms. You can reference back to this chapter if any terms confuse you along the way. The terms are organized into three separate categories (candy making tools, terms used in making candy, and recurring ingredients) to help identify what they are used for.

Candy Making Tools

Blender:

A traditional kitchen appliances that is able to mix, blend, and puree ingredients.

Candy Thermometer:

A crucial tool used to measure the temperature while making candy. Although there are many types of candy thermometers, it is recommended that you purchase one with a clip to avoid it from falling into the mixture.

Food Processor:

A kitchen appliance used for food preparation. For candy making, the food processor serves a similar purpose as a blender in pureeing the needed ingredients.

Heat Resistant Gloves:

Used to protect the hands from hot surfaces. Making candy requires dealing with stovetops and ovens. You will also handle many hot mixtures and these gloves should be able to protect you from accidentally burning yourself.

Kitchen Scissors:

Similar to regular scissors, these scissors were made to deal with food. It will help you break the candy into pieces before serving.

Measuring Cup:

To follow the required amount of ingredients that a recipe suggests, it is important to have measuring cups.

Microwave:

A common kitchen appliance used to heat up food. When making candy, microwaves can be of great use when the mixture has hardened and you need a quick fix to soften it back down.

Mold:

Assists in shaping the candy. Most recipes require the hot candy mixture to be put into molds to set. You can also customize the appearances of your candy by choosing unique designs.

Parchment Paper:

Serves as a disposable nonstick surface. It allows the mixtures to be easily separated from a pan. It can also have a double purpose as a candy wrapper.

Pastry Brush:

A secret tool or technique used when cooking sugar. It is usually used wet with water to remove any unwanted seed crystals from the side of the pan. It is important to get rid of seed crystals since they may cause the candy to turn out grainy. It is recommended that you purchase one with rubber bristles.

Rubber Spatula:

A multi-purpose kitchen tool that can help spread, even out, or scoop mixtures. It has a rubber tip to gently handle mixtures.

Saucepan:

A type of pan usually used for deep cooking. It has an elongated handle and a lid. It is recommendable to find one with a thick bottom as it will decrease chances of burning the candy.

Skewer:

Although generally used when barbecuing, these kitchen tools can be used to puncture holes inside the candy so you can hang them from a string.

Syringe:

Transferring mixtures from saucepan to molds can be difficult. This tool can accurately pour the mixture into a mold without having to worry about spilling.

Timer:

Some recipes require multi-tasking. In those cases, it is easy to lose track of time and may cause your candy to overcook. Timers are great prevention towards that.

Whisk:

A kitchen tool used to help smooth out mixtures. It can also help speed up the process of dissolving certain ingredients.

Terms Used in Making Candy

If you are new to making candy, here is a list of terms you can familiarize yourself with.

Blooming:

The process of letting the agar agar absorb the water for 3 to 5 minutes. This allows it to dissolve evenly when heat is applied. Blooming lets the candies have a smooth texture.

Hard Crack Stage:

Refers to when a sugar mixture is around 300 to 310 degrees F. In case you don't have a candy thermometer, you can use the traditional trick technique of dropping a small amount of the mixture in cold water. Remove the candy from the water and try to break it. If it cracks, it has reached the hard crack stage.

Heaping:

When measuring an ingredient (usually a powder), a heaping amount calls for a large scoop. It should still be able to fit the required amount, but excessive enough to form a small pile on top of the spoon.

Knead:

To work, massage, or mix using your hands. By kneading the candy, you are increasing its elasticity. It also makes it easier to consume.

Score:

Creating cuts in the candy with a sharp knife. Scoring a candy is usually used to help shape the candy. The cuts are generally shallow but should be deep enough to use as a guideline when breaking the candy.

Sift:

This process involves filtering ingredients through a fine mesh strainer. It is important while making candy since it will make the ingredients easier to mix. It will also get rid of any unwanted chunks.

Simmer:

The stage in cooking where a liquid is kept just below boiling point. Simmering is characterized as letting the mixture have gentle bubbles while cooking.

Soft Ball Stage:

Refers to when the sugar mixture has reached a temperature of 234 to 240 degrees F. If you don't have a candy thermometer, you can drop the mixture into cold water. If you are able to form a flexible ball after removing it from the water, it has reached the soft ball stage.

Recurring Ingredients

All of the ingredients listed below are commonly used in the candy recipes to follow. Most of these terms listed below are great plant based alternatives and can be equipped in other dishes besides candy.

Aquafaba:

The liquid leftover from chickpeas. It is the vegan alternative for egg whites.

Agar Agar:

A jelly like substance made from red algae or seaweed. It is a vegan alternative for gelatin.

Coconut Milk:

The liquid squeezed from coconut meat. It adds creaminess to any vegan dish.

Cream of Tartar:

A byproduct when making wine or grape juice. It helps to thicken the mixture.

Flavoring Oil:

Gives the candy a boost in flavor. They also help make the candy smell like the desired flavor.

Food Coloring:

Aids in dying the candy. It serves as a type of decor to your candies and therefore more attractive.

Fruit Juice:

Helps achieve a natural, healthy flavor to the candies. It also helps with the pigment of the candy.

Liquid Stevia Extract:

Derived from a sweet tasting plant called Stevia. It is a healthier alternative to sugar.

Maple Syrup:

A syrup made from the sap of a maple tree. Because of its similar consistency, it is a vegan alternative for honey.

Soy Milk:

A by product of soaking and grinding soy beans. It is a common vegan alternative for milk.

Turmeric:

Typically used to not only warm the colors of the food, but to warm the flavors as well. It has as similar taste to ginger. It usually comes in a powder form.

Vegan Butter/Margarine:

Instead of using regular butter, vegan margarine is a mix of vegetable fat and water. It can be used to coat pans to make them have a nonstick surface.

CHAPTER 3:

VEGAN CANDY RECIPES

This chapter contains a mixture of hard and gummy candy, along with a few of our other favorite candy recipes!

Hard Candy: Although many store bought candies identify as vegan, it is arguable to say that there's more joy in making these candies yourself. Not only do they cost less to make, but they allow you to share more with friends and family. From lollipops to seasonal candy, here are plenty of hard candies you can try.

Gummy Candy: Unlike the hard candies, it is difficult to find gummy candy that is vegan. This is because a majority of gummies use gelatin. However, the gummy candy recipes below utilize plant based ingredients. Feel free to make the following candies that are not only delicious to eat, but also provide a sweet and healthy option.

JOLLY RANCHERS

Serves: 12

Nutritional Information (per serving):
Calories: 13 | Carbohydrates: 3.3g | Fats: 0g | Protein: 0g

INGREDIENTS:

- 1 cup xylitol
- 1/4 tsp watermelon oil
- 1/3 cup brewed strawberry tea
- 1/2 to 3 tsp citric acid powder

EQUIPMENT:

- Candy mold

DIRECTIONS:

1. Turn the stove on high heat. In a medium sized saucepan, pour in the xylitol and brewed tea. When it reaches 300 degrees F, remove it from the heat.
2. Stir in the watermelon oil and your preferred amount of citric acid powder. Keep in mind that the more citric acid you put in, the more sour the candies will be.
3. Pour the mixture into candy molds.
4. Place in the fridge overnight.

LOLLIPOPS

Serves: 8

Nutritional Information (per serving):
Calories: 158 | Carbohydrates: 41g | Fats: 0g | Protein: 0g

INGREDIENTS:

- 1 cup sugar
- 1/2 cup light corn syrup
- 1/4 cup water
- 1 1/2 tsp of almond extract
- Food coloring
- Nonstick cooking spray

EQUIPMENT:

- Lollipop sticks
- Lollipop mold

DIRECTIONS:

1. With nonstick cooking spray, lightly spritz each lollipop mold. Dab the inside of the mold with a paper towel to get rid of any excess oil.
2. Place the lollipop sticks into the mold.
3. Mix the sugar, light corn syrup, and water in the saucepan. Set the heat to medium high.
4. Keep stirring the mixture until the sugar has dissolved. Use a damp pastry brush to clean the sides of the pan.
5. When the mixture has reached its boiling point, put in the candy thermometer. Avoid stirring as it boils.
6. After it has reached 300 degrees F, remove the pan from the stove. Add in the extract and food coloring.
7. Carefully scoop the liquid into the lollipop molds. Make sure the lollipop sticks are completely coated.
8. Store in the refrigerator overnight.

CANDY CORN

Serves: 100

Nutritional Information (per serving):
Calories: 25.8 | Carbohydrates: 6.6g | Fats: 0g | Protein: 0g

INGREDIENTS:

- 1 cup sugar
- 2/3 cup corn syrup
- 5 tbsp vegan margarine
- 1 tsp vanilla extract
- 2 1/2 cup powdered sugar
- 1/3 cup powdered soy milk
- 1 pinch of salt
- Yellow food coloring
- Red food coloring

DIRECTIONS:

1. Mix the sugar, margarine, vanilla, and corn syrup in a large saucepan until it boils.
2. Decrease the heat to medium. Let the mixture boil for about five minutes, while stirring occasionally. Then, remove it from the heat.
3. In a bowl, sift the powdered sugar, powdered soy milk, and salt consecutively.
4. Combine the powder mixture with the hot mixture. Stir thoroughly until the ingredients have completely mixed. You should be left with a dough like consistency.
5. Leave it to cool until it is slightly warm. This should take approximately 15 minutes.
6. Separate the dough into three identical pieces. Knead one of the thirds until smooth.
7. With the second piece, add about 8 drops of yellow food coloring and knead until smooth.
8. For the third piece, add about 6 drops of yellow food

coloring and 2 drops of red food coloring to achieve an orange pigment. Knead until smooth. If the dough starts to become too stiff to work with, put it in the microwave for 10 seconds.

9. Roll each piece into a roll until they have reached an identical size. These rolls shouldn't be thinner than 1/4 inch. Then lay the white, orange, and yellow ropes next to each other and press them to form one piece.

10. To form the shape of a candy corn, cut out the dough diagonally. Each slice should face an alternate direction to create the shape of a triangle.

POP ROCKS

Serves: 16

Nutritional Information (per serving):
Calories: 128 | Carbohydrates: 33g | Fats: 0g | Protein: 0g

INGREDIENTS:

- 1 pinch of corn starch
- 2 cup sugar
- 1 tsp baking soda
- 1/4 cup and 1 tsp citric acid
- 1/2 cup light corn syrup
- 1/4 cup water
- 1 tsp your choice of extract
- 1-2 drops of your choice of food coloring

EQUIPMENT:

- Baking pan

DIRECTIONS:

1. Start by sprinkling a baking pan with a pinch of corn starch.
2. Combine the sugar, corn syrup, and water in a medium sized saucepan. Continue cooking the concoction until it reaches 300 degrees F. Then, remove the pan from the heat.
3. While it is still hot, add the baking soda, 1/4 cup citric acid, extract, and food coloring. Keep mixing until all ingredients have dissolved.
4. Pour out the mixture evenly on a baking pan, making sure that it doesn't pass the edges. Dust the flat, evenly distributed mixture with 1 tsp citric acid.
5. Leave the candy too cool for approximately 30 minutes.
6. When it has hardened, crack the candy into pieces and

place them into a resealable plastic bag. With a rolling pin, break the candy into smaller pieces.

STAINED GLASS CANDY

Serves: 1

Nutritional Information (per serving):
Calories: 1874.7 | Carbohydrates: 487.1g | Fats: 0.2g | Protein: 0g

INGREDIENTS:

- 2 cup sugar
- 1/3 cup light corn syrup
- 1/3 cup water
- 2 tbsp vinegar
- 3 drops of peppermint oil
- Food coloring

EQUIPMENT:

- Candy mold

DIRECTIONS:

1. Start by mixing sugar, syrup, water, and vinegar in a saucepan. Stir the mixture on medium heat until it has reached the hard crack stage of 300 degrees F.
2. Immediately remove it from the heat. Add in the peppermint oil. Let the candy sit until it has slightly cooled down.
3. Carefully pour the mixture into candy molds. Then add minimal drops of food coloring onto each mold. Use a toothpick to spread delicately.
4. After it hardens, you can pop it out of the mold.

LEMON DROPS

Serves: 1

Nutritional Information (per serving):
Calories: 28 | Carbohydrates: 7g | Fats: 0g | Protein: 0g

INGREDIENTS:

- 1 cup fresh lemon juice
- 1 cup sugar

EQUIPMENT:

- Candy mold

DIRECTIONS:

1. In a bowl, combine the sugar and fresh lemon juice together. Continue mixing until the sugar has completely dissolved.
2. Boil the mixture in a pan on medium high heat. Stir continuously until you have reached a thick consistency. This will usually take 20-30 minutes. To check if the mixture is ready, drop a small amount into cold water. If it hardens, it's good to go.
3. Using a cooking syringe, transfer the mixture from the bowl onto small silicon molds.
4. Place inside the refrigerator to cool for about an hour or two.

FUNFETTI SALTWATER TAFFY

Serves: 50

Nutritional Information (per serving):
Calories: 32 | Carbohydrates: 7g | Fats: 3.5g | Protein: 0g

INGREDIENTS:

- 1 cup sugar
- 1 tbsp cornstarch
- 2/3 cup light corn syrup
- 1 tbsp vegan butter + extra for kneading
- 1/2 cup water
- 1/2 tsp salt
- 1 tbsp vanilla bean paste
- Rainbow sprinkles
- nonstick cooking spray

EQUIPMENT:

- Baking pan

DIRECTIONS:

1. Prepare a baking pan by lightly greasing it with nonstick cooking spray.
2. Using a medium saucepan, add in the sugar, cornstarch, light corn syrup, vegan butter, water, and salt. Set the heat to medium high heat. Mix it thoroughly.
3. Using a candy thermometer, keep track of the mixture's temperature. When it has reached 255 degrees F, remove it from the heat.
4. Stir in the vanilla bean paste. Then pour the hot mixture onto the baking pan.
5. Add the rainbow sprinkles to the mixture. Make sure to cover all parts of the taffy.
6. Wait until the taffy is cool enough to touch. Rub vegan butter on your hands and create a ball with the taffy.

Knead and stretch the taffy for about 15 minutes. This will make the candy chewier.

7. Form the taffy into a rope. Use kitchen scissors (lightly greased) to cut the taffy into smaller pieces.

CANDY CANES

Serves: 18

Nutritional Information (per serving):
Calories: 182 | Carbohydrates: 48g | Fats: 0g | Protein: 0g

INGREDIENTS:

- 3 cup sugar
- 1 cup light corn syrup
- 1/2 cup water
- 1 1/2 tsps peppermint extract
- 1 tsp red food coloring gel
- 1 tsp white food coloring gel
- Nonstick cooking spray

EQUIPMENT:

- Baking pan

DIRECTIONS:

1. Lightly spray 2 baking pans with nonstick cooking spray.
2. Prepare the oven by preheating it to 200 degrees F.
3. Mix the sugar, light corn syrup, and 1/4 cup water in a medium sized saucepan. Bring it over medium high heat. Keep mixing until the sugar has dissolved.
4. With the rest of the water and a wet pastry brush, remove any crystals that start to form on the sides of the pan. Refrain from stirring the mixture.
5. Once the mixture has boiled, insert a candy thermometer into the pan. Let it boil until it has reached its soft crack stage at 285 degrees F.
6. Take the pan off the heat. Wait for the bubbles to die down, then mix in the peppermint extract.
7. Pour half of the mixture onto a prepared baking pan. Then, place it in the preheated oven.

8. Stir the red food coloring in the remaining mixture of syrup. Add more food coloring to achieve a more vibrant color.
9. Transfer the mixture onto the remaining baking pan. Let it sit until it develops a "skin".
10. Coat a metal spatula with nonstick cooking spray. Use it to knead the red candy. Do this for 1 to 2 minutes.
11. Put on a pair of heat resistant gloves. Pull the candy into a rope, fold the rope in half, then twist. Repeat this process for 2 to 3 minutes. Doing so will cause the candy to have a satiny appearance.
12. Stretch candy back into a rope, about 2 inches wide. Then, put it inside the oven.
13. Remove the other batch of candy from the oven. Carefully knead in the white food coloring using the metal spatula from earlier.
14. Repeat the same process as you did with the red candy: pull, fold, and twist for 2 to 3 minutes.
15. Form the white candy into a rope about 2 inches wide.
16. Remove the red candy from the oven. Cut 2 inches off of the white and red rope.
17. Lay the red and white candy horizontally. Press them together so that they merge into one. The red candy should be on top, while the white is on bottom.
18. Twist the rope to fulfill the candy cane's traditional stripes. Form a hook before the candy solidifies.
19. Continue the process until you have used up all the candy.

WATERMELON CANDY

Serves: 5

Nutritional Information (per serving):
Calories: 21 | Carbohydrates: 5g | Fats: 0g | Protein: 0g

INGREDIENTS:

- 1 1/2 fresh watermelon

EQUIPMENT:

- Dehydrator

DIRECTIONS:

1. Separate the watermelon rind. Then cut the watermelon into strips. Try to make them as even as possible.
2. Lay the watermelon strips onto dehydrator sheets.
3. Set the food dehydrator to 125 degrees F.
4. After you have set the strips inside the dehydrator, set the timer to 6 to 8 hours. Continue checking on it every couple of hours.

CARAMEL CHEWS

Serves: 32

Nutritional Information (per serving):
Calories: 142 | Carbohydrates: 21g | Fats: 6g | Protein: 0g

INGREDIENTS:

- 1 cup vegan butter spread
- 2 cup light brown sugar
- 1 cup light corn syrup
- 1/3 tsp sea salt
- 11 oz full fat coconut milk

EQUIPMENT:

- Baking pan

DIRECTIONS:

1. Start by laying a piece of parchment paper on a rimmed baking pan.
2. In a saucepan, melt the vegan spread over medium high heat. You can also attach a candy thermometer to check on the temperature of the mixture.
3. Once it has melted, add the light brown sugar and continue to stir until it has dissolved.
4. Pour the light corn syrup and coconut milk into the mixture.
5. Let the mixture boil, while stirring continuously to avoid the caramel from burning. When it has reached 235 degrees F, the caramel has reached the soft ball stage. This process usually takes 15 to 20 minutes.
6. Remove the pan from heat. Stir in the sea salt.
7. Spread the hot caramel evenly on the tray. You can also use a rubber spatula to help.

8. Cool off the caramel before slicing. Then, you cut the caramel into smaller squares.
9. You can also opt to individually wrap each caramel square in wax or parchment paper.

CINNAMON ROCK CANDY

Serves: 1

Nutritional Information (per serving):
Calories: 126 | Carbohydrates: 33g | Fats: 0g | Protein: 0g

INGREDIENTS:

- 2 cup sugar
- 1 cup water
- 1/2 cup light corn syrup
- 1/4 or 1/2 tsp cinnamon oil
- 1/2 tsp red food coloring

EQUIPMENT:

- Baking pan

DIRECTIONS:

1. Using a large saucepan on medium heat, mix the sugar, water, and corn syrup together. Cover and leave the mixture to cook for three minutes, while stirring occasionally.
2. When it has boiled, turn up the heat to medium high. Check the temperature of the mixture with a candy thermometer. When it reaches 310 degrees F, it has reached the hard crack stage.
3. Remove the pan from the heat. Carefully add in the cinnamon oil and food coloring. Remember to take precaution with this step as the smell of the mixture may be intense.
4. While it is still hot, pour it onto the greased baking pan. With a sharp knife, you can score the cinnamon block into smaller squares. Leave it to cool at room temperature until it becomes dry.

5. Use a knife to cut the block into squares, using the scores you made earlier as guidelines.

CANDY BUTTONS

Serves: 10

Nutritional Information (per serving):
Calories: 104 | Carbohydrates: 26g | Fats: 0g | Protein: 0g

INGREDIENTS:

- 2 cup confectioners' sugar
- 4 1/2 tsps vegan meringue powder
- 1/4 cup water
- 1/4 tsp vanilla extract
- Red food coloring
- Blue food coloring
- Green food coloring

DIRECTIONS:

1. Prepare 10 strips of parchment paper. Each should measure 16 inches long and 2 inches wide.
2. Sift both confectioners' sugar and vegan meringue powder into a bowl. Mix in the water and vanilla extract thoroughly.
3. Prepare 3 smaller bowls. Distribute the mixture in each bowl equally. Then make each mixture a different color using food coloring.
4. Attach a #3 pastry tip onto a pastry bag. Then, fill the bag with one mixture. Carefully pipe a circle the size of a penny onto the parchment paper until it runs out. Continue the process until you have gone through all three bowls.
5. Let the buttons dry and harden, which should take about 8 hours.

MERINGUE

Serves: 66

Nutritional Information (per serving):
Calories: 6 | Carbohydrates: 1.5g | Fats: 0g | Protein: 0g

INGREDIENTS:

- 6 tbsp aquafaba
- 1/4 tsp cream of tartar
- 1/2 cup white sugar
- 1/2 tsp vanilla extract

EQUIPMENT:

- Baking pan

DIRECTIONS:

1. Combine the aquafaba and cream of tartar with an electric mixer. Begin the mixing at a slow speed and continue mixing until its consistency is foamy.
2. Slowly increase the mixer's speed until the mixture is white and is able to form stiff peaks and is meringue like.
3. As the mixer works at a fast speed, slowly add the sugar and vanilla extract.
4. Prepare the oven by preheating it to 250 degrees F.
5. Set a piece of parchment paper on a baking pan.
6. Take the bowl of meringue mix and transfer it to a baking pan with a spoon.
7. Place into the oven for about 45 minutes. Do not open the oven door.

PEPPERMINT HARD CANDIES

Serves: 1

Nutritional Information (per serving):
Calories: 261 | Carbohydrates: 65g | Fats: 1g | Protein: 0g

INGREDIENTS:

- 1 tbsp vegan butter
- 2 cup sugar
- 1 cup light corn syrup
- 1 1/2 tsp peppermint extract
- 1 tsp vanilla extract
- 6 - 8 drops of green food coloring

EQUIPMENT:

- Baking pan

DIRECTIONS:

1. Use foil to line a baking pan. Use the vegan butter to lightly coat the foil.
2. With a large saucepan, mix the sugar and light corn syrup together. Bring the mixture to a boil, while set on medium heat. Stir the mixture occasionally.
3. Cover the pan and let the mixture cook for 3 minutes. This will help to dissolve the sugar.
4. Uncover the pan and increase the heat to medium high. Place a candy thermometer to observe the temperature.
5. When it has reached 300 degrees F, remove it from the heat. Add in the food coloring and extracts.
6. Transfer the mixture from saucepan to baking pan. Let it cool, then break it into shards.

TRADITIONAL DIVINITY CANDY

Serves: 40

Nutritional Information (per serving):
Calories: 31 | Carbohydrates: 3g | Fats: 3.4g | Protein: 1g

INGREDIENTS:

- 2 1/2 cup sugar
- 1/2 cup water
- 1/2 cup light corn syrup
- 1/8 tsp salt
- 4 tbsp aquafaba, room temperature
- 1 cup chopped pecans
- 1 tsp vanilla extract

EQUIPMENT:

- Baking pan

DIRECTIONS:

1. Prepare a baking pan with parchment paper and set it aside.
2. With a large saucepan, mix the sugar, corn syrup, water, and salt. Let it cook over medium heat, while stirring occasionally.
3. When the mixture starts to boil, insert a candy thermometer in the mixture. Avoid stirring the mixture until it has reached 260 degrees F.
4. While waiting for the mixture to reach the set temperature, start whipping the aquafaba. Use a mixer with a paddle attachment and set it to high speed. Continue mixing until the aquafaba is fully whipped.
5. After the mixture has reached 260 degrees F, remove the pan from the heat. Carefully pour it into the bowl of aquafaba while mixing. Be sure to do this slowly as the

hot liquid may splatter. Pouring the entire mixture into the bowl should take around 2 minutes.

6. Continue to beat the mixture for around 5 to 8 minutes. Check for when the candy is firm enough by placing a small amount on the parchment paper. If it can stand without melting into a puddle, you can move onto the next step. If it cannot, continue beating for about 1 to 2 minutes.

7. Add the chopped pecans and vanilla to the mixture.

8. Spray two spoons lightly with cooking spray. Then, scoop tbsp sized drops of the candy onto the parchment paper. Use the other spoon to help scrape off the excess. Do this quickly before the candy cools down.

9. Let the candy set.

BURNT SUGAR LOLLIPOPS

Serves: 24

Nutritional Information (per serving):
Calories: 86 | Carbohydrates: 22.5g | Fats: 9.5g | Protein: 0g

INGREDIENTS:

- 2 cup sugar
- 1/2 cup light corn syrup
- 1/4 cup water
- 1/4 tsp cream of tartar
- 24 cinnamon sticks, at least 4 inches long

EQUIPMENT:

- Baking pan

DIRECTIONS:

1. Prepare a large baking pan and line it with parchment paper. Let it chill in the refrigerator for about 30 minutes.
2. While waiting, combine the sugar, corn syrup, water, and cream of tartar together in a medium saucepan. Set the heat to medium and stir for about 3 minutes, or until the sugar has melted.
3. Let the mixture simmer by raising the heat to medium high. Use a wet pastry brush to brush down any crystals on the side of the pan. Do this for 5 minutes.
4. The mixture should reach a boil and turn a light amber pigment. Remove it from the heat.
5. Let the mixture sit for around 2 minutes.
6. Remove the chilled tray from the refrigerator. Pour the mixture onto the parchment paper while forming 1 1/2 inch circles. Be mindful of the distance between each drop you make.

7. Lay down and press a cinnamon stick into each circle. Drizzle another layer of the mixture on top of the cinnamon stick to seal.
8. Let it cool for about 20 minutes.

BUTTERSCOTCH

Serves: 64

Nutritional Information (per serving):
Calories: 83 | Carbohydrates: 8g | Fats: 3g | Protein: 0g

INGREDIENTS:

- 1 lb sugar
- 1 lb unsalted vegan butter
- 4 oz vegan molasses
- 10 - 14 g sea salt
- nonstick cooking spray

EQUIPMENT:

- Baking pan

DIRECTIONS:

1. Prepare the baking pan by lining it with nonstick foil. Make sure the foil goes up and over the opposite sides of the pan. Spray nonstick cooking spray all over the pan, especially on the other two sides that aren't covered. Then, set it aside.
2. Use a medium saucepan to melt the vegan butter over medium low heat.
3. Add in the molasses, sugar, and salt.
4. When the mixture has a liquid - like consistency, turn up the heat to medium high. Stir it occasionally as you wait for it to boil.
5. Leave the candy on the stove until it reaches 250 degrees F. Pour the mixture slowly into the pan you prepared earlier.
6. Let it cool down until warm. Use a sharp knife to score the butterscotch. Glide a small rubber spatula in between

the butterscotch and the pan on the sides that aren't covered with foil.

7. Place it in the refrigerator to completely cool. Then, cut and serve.

MANGO CHILI CANDIES

Serves: 24

Nutritional Information (per serving):
Calories: 48 | Carbohydrates: 12g | Fats: 0g | Protein: 0g

INGREDIENTS:

- 1 cup sugar
- 1 cup mango nectar
- 1/4 cup light corn syrup
- 1/2 tsp mango candy flavoring
- 1 tbsp Tajin Clasico seasoning
- Nonstick cooking spray

EQUIPMENT:

- Candy mold

DIRECTIONS:

1. Spritz the candy molds with nonstick cooking spray.
2. Mix the sugar, mango nectar, and corn syrup in a large saucepan. Let the mixture boil on medium high heat.
3. Let the mixture stay on the heat until it reaches the hard crack stage of 275 degrees F. Then, remove the pan from the heat.
4. Add in the mango candy flavoring and stir the mixture thoroughly.
5. Pour the candy into the mold halfway. Sprinkle in the Tajin spice into each mold, then fill the rest of the mold with the mango candy mixture.
6. Let the candies set for about 15 minutes. Remove them from the molds, and serve.

SEEDLESS WATERMELON HARD CANDY

Serves: 40

Nutritional Information (per serving):
Calories: 19 | Carbohydrates: 5g | Fats: 0g | Protein: 0g

INGREDIENTS:

- 1 cup sugar
- 1 cup water
- Red food coloring
- Watermelon flavored essence

EQUIPMENT:

- Baking pan

DIRECTIONS:

1. Lay a piece of parchment paper on a small pan.
2. In a small saucepan, combine the sugar and water together on medium heat. Constantly stir the mixture until it boils.
3. Cover the pan and allow the mixture to boil for 3 to 5 minutes. Remove the cover and insert the candy thermometer. Remove it from the heat when it reaches 310 degrees F.
4. Let the mix sit for 30 seconds to a minute. Stir in drops of red food coloring, along with the watermelon flavoring.
5. Pour the warm mixture onto the parchment paper - lined pan.
6. Let it cool at room temperature for around 4 minutes. At that point, the candy should be firm but soft enough to cut through.
7. Use kitchen scissors to cut the candy into any shape you'd

like. Then you can dust the candies with a light layer of powdered sugar to prevent the candies from sticking onto one another.

GUMMY BEARS

Serves: 50

Nutritional Information (per serving):
Calories: 21 | Carbohydrates: 5g | Fats: 2.3g | Protein: 0g

INGREDIENTS:

- 1/2 cup any fruit juice
- 2 tbsp agar agar powder
- 1 - 2 tbsp sugar

EQUIPMENT:

- Gummy bear mold

DIRECTIONS:

1. Combine all of the ingredients into a medium sized saucepan. Set the heat to low, while slowly stirring the mixture until it reaches a thicker consistency. This should take about 1 to 2 minutes.
2. Using a spoon, pour the mixture into the gummy bear molds.
3. Place the mold in the freezer for 5 minutes.
4. Pop the gummy bears from the molds.

BLUEBERRY GUMMIES

Serves: 70

Nutritional Information (per serving):
Calories: 7 | Fats: 0.7g | Carbohydrates: 1g | Protein: 0g

INGREDIENTS:

- 1 1/2 cup water
- 2 1/2 cup blueberries
- 6 tbsp fresh lemon juice
- 1/4 cup maple syrup
- 1/2 cup agar agar
- Nonstick cooking spray

EQUIPMENT:

- Baking pan

DIRECTIONS:

1. Prepare the baking pan with nonstick cooking spray. Wipe off any excess, then set aside.
2. With a blender, combine the water, blueberries, lemon juice, and maple syrup. Continue to blend until there are no more chunks.
3. Pour the smoothie into a small saucepan. Heat the mixture until it slightly simmers.
4. Use a whisk to stir in the agar agar. Don't stop mixing until the agar agar has fully mixed.
5. Remove from the heat and pour into the prepared pan.
6. Let the pan cool down to room temperature. This should take about an hour.
7. Place it in the refrigerator for 2 to 4 hours for the mixture to firm.
8. Take the pan out of the refrigerator. Use a knife to cut into smaller squares.

PEACH MANGO GUMMIES

Serves: 36

Nutritional Information (per serving):
Calories: 40 | Carbohydrates: 3g | Fats: 4.4g | Protein: 0g

INGREDIENTS:

- 4 packets of Lipton Peach Mango Herbal Tea
- 1 1/2 cup hot water
- 8 oz frozen and unsweetened peaches
- 1/3 cup lemon juice
- 6 tbsp agar agar
- 1/4 tsp liquid stevia extract

EQUIPMENT:

- Gummy mold

DIRECTIONS:

1. Get all four packets of the peach mango tea and brew it in the hot water for about 5 minutes. Then, remove the tea bags. Make sure to squeeze out any excess liquid from the tea bags.
2. Using a blender, pour in the peaches and lemon juice. Then add the hot peach mango tea. Blend until you have achieved a smooth consistency.
3. Transfer the mixture to a saucepan. Scatter the agar agar into the saucepan. Let it sit for about 5 minutes.
4. Put the saucepan on medium high heat. Whisk the mixture occasionally. Take it off the heat when bubbles start to form.
5. Mix in the liquid stevia extract with a whisk.
6. Pour the mixture carefully into the gummy molds. Scrape

off any excess. Then let the gummies cool at room temperature for about an hour.

7. Place the pan in the fridge overnight or until they are firm.

PROBIOTIC GUMMY CANDY

Serves: 40

Nutritional Information (per serving):
Calories: 27 | Carbohydrates: 4g | Fats: 1g | Protein: 1g

INGREDIENTS:

- 1 cup coconut milk
- 1 cup fruit puree
- 1/2 - 1 cup maple syrup
- 1/2 cup agar agar
- 1 pinch of sea salt
- 8 - 10 capsules of probiotics, removed from capsules
- 1 tbsp vanilla extract
- Beet juice as food coloring

EQUIPMENT:

- Candy mold

DIRECTIONS:

1. In a saucepan, combine the coconut milk, maple syrup, and salt. Heat it until it simmers.
2. Gradually add in the agar agar by sprinkling it on to the mixture. Whisk it until it has fully dissolved.
3. Remove the pan from the heat. Let the mixture cool down until it has reached 105 to 110 degrees F. Within this temperature range, you won't be able to kill the antibiotics.
4. Combine the fruit puree, vanilla extract, probiotics, and beet juice with the mixture.
5. Transfer the mixture to candy molds. Leave it to cool and solidify in the refrigerator for around 30 minutes to an hour.

LEMON FLAVORED GUMMIES

Serves: 32

Nutritional Information (per serving):
Calories: 50 | Carbohydrates: 6g | Fats: 0g | Protein: 6g

INGREDIENTS:

- 1 1/2 cup lemon juice
- 3/4 cup unsweetened apple sauce
- 1/2 tsp ground turmeric
- 6 tbsp agar agar
- 1 tsp liquid stevia extract
- 1/2 tsp lemon flavoring

EQUIPMENT:

- Gummy bear mold

DIRECTIONS:

1. In a saucepan, combine the lemon juice, apple sauce, and turmeric together.
2. Scatter the agar agar on top of the mixture. Leave it to sit for about 5 minutes until it absorbs all the liquid.
3. Place the saucepan on medium high heat. Whisk occasionally until the mixture turns smooth. When the agar agar has completely melted, remove pan from the heat.
4. Mix in the liquid stevia extract and lemon flavoring with the whisk.
5. Fill the gummy bear mold with the mixture. Let it sit for an hour, then refrigerate overnight.

GUMDROPS

Serves: 10

Nutritional Information (per serving):
Calories: 66 | Carbohydrates: 17g | Fats: 0g | Protein: 0g

INGREDIENTS:

- 3/4 cup water
- 1/3 cup sugar
- 3/4 tsp agar agar
- 1/8 tsp green food color
- 1/8 tsp red food color
- 1/2 cup sugar, to coat
- 1/4 tsp orange essence

EQUIPMENT:

- Gumdrop candy mold

DIRECTIONS:

1. Combine the water, sugar, and agar agar in a saucepan.
2. Let the mixture simmer for 5 minutes. Make sure to stir it occasionally so that the agar agar doesn't stick to the bottom of the pan.
3. Add the orange essence to the mixture.
4. Evenly distribute the mixture into 2 bowls. Add a different color of food coloring to each bowl and then mix.
5. Pour the mixture into the mold. Leave it to cool in the refrigerator for about 4 hours.
6. Remove the gumdrops from the mold carefully.
7. Put half a cup sugar on a plate and coat the gumdrops generously. Let it sit for 24 hours on a tray lined with parchment paper.
8. Coat the gumdrops with sugar for the second time. Leave it to sit for another 24 hours for the sugar to crystallize.

ORANGE CREAMSICLE GUMMY CANDY

Serves: 30

Nutritional Information (per serving):
Calories: 25 | Carbohydrates: 5.7g | Fats: 0.4g | Protein: 0.3g

INGREDIENTS:

- 2 cup orange juice
- 1 cup coconut milk
- 2 tbsp maple syrup
- 1/2 tsp vanilla extract
- 3 tbsp agar agar

EQUIPMENT:

- Candy mold

DIRECTIONS:

1. Start by mixing orange juice, coconut milk, maple syrup, vanilla extract, and agar agar in a medium saucepan.
2. Heat the mixture over medium high heat. It should simmer for about 2 minutes.
3. Remove the gummy mixture from the heat. Pour the mixture into a mold.
4. Refrigerate the gummy candy for at least 30 minutes to fully solidify.

FRUIT ROLL CANDY

Serves: 1

Nutritional Information (per serving):
Calories: 64 | Carbohydrates: 16g | Fats: 7.1g | Protein: 0g

INGREDIENTS:

- 2 cup strawberries
- 1 cup blackberries
- 2 tbsp maple syrup
- 1 tsp fresh lemon juice

EQUIPMENT:

- Baking pan

DIRECTIONS:

1. Start by preheating your oven to 140 degrees F. Then, line a baking pan with parchment paper.
2. Bring out a blender or a food processor. Puree the strawberries, blackberries, maple syrup, and lemon juice until there are no chunks.
3. Pour the mixture on the baking pan, making sure that it is evenly spread. Do your best to make it thin without causing holes.
4. Put the tray inside the oven for 4 to 6 hours. Observe the fruit roll every 30 minutes. You will know it's ready to take out of the oven when the texture isn't sticky.
5. Remove the tray from the oven. Let the fruit roll cool down, then remove it from the parchment paper.

RASPBERRY CHOCOLATE GUMMY BEARS

Serves: 4

Nutritional Information (per serving):
Calories: 37 | Carbohydrates: 3g | Fats: 0g | Protein: 7g

INGREDIENTS:

For the raspberry gummies:

- 1/2 cup boiling water
- 1/2 cup fresh raspberries
- 1 tbsp agar agar
- 10 -15 drops of liquid stevia extract

For the chocolate gummies:

- 1/2 cup boiling water
- 1 tbsp agar agar
- 1 1/2 tbsp cocoa powder
- 10 - 15 drops of liquid stevia extract

EQUIPMENT:

- Candy mold

DIRECTIONS:

To make the raspberry gummies:

1. Pour the hot water into a bowl. Add the fresh raspberries and crush them until all the juice is released.
2. Grab a mesh strainer and filter the mixture. This will help get rid of any unwanted seeds.
3. If the temperature of the liquid is still warm, you can mix in the agar agar gradually. If the liquid has cooled down, you can pop it in the microwave for 10 seconds. The hotter the liquid is, the easier the agar agar will dissolve.

4. Stir the mixture until you have gotten rid of all chunks. Add the drops of liquid stevia extract to taste.
5. Pour the raspberry mixture into candy molds, but only halfway. Leave the mixture to cool in the refrigerator.

To make the chocolate gummies:

1. With a clean bowl, add half a cup boiling water. Slowly add in the agar agar while constantly stirring.
2. Combine cocoa powder and the desired amount of liquid stevia extract to the mixture. Mix thoroughly.

To combine:

1. Retrieve the candy molds from the refrigerator. Check to see that the layer of raspberry candy has solidified.
2. Fill the molds with a chocolate layer until they are full. Return the candies to the fridge and let cool for 15 to 20 minutes.
3. Remove the mold from the refrigerator and pop out the candy.

CHERRY LIME GUMMY CANDY

Serves: 16

Nutritional Information (per serving):
Calories: 19 | Carbohydrates: 3g | Fats: 2g | Protein: 1g

INGREDIENTS:

- 3/4 cup 100% organic tart cherry juice
- 1/4 cup fresh lime juice
- 2 tbsp maple syrup
- 3 tbsp agar agar

EQUIPMENT:

- Gummy mold

DIRECTIONS:

1. Combine the cherry and lime juice in a saucepan. Set the heat to medium and bring it to a simmer.
2. Lower the heat to the lowest setting possible. Stir in the maple syrup and mix thoroughly with a whisk.
3. Gradually add in the agar agar. Make sure that it is fully dissolved by constantly whisking it. This should take around 10 minutes.
4. Remove the mixture from the heat and transfer it to the gummy molds.
5. Leave the candy in the refrigerator to solidify.

RED HOT CINNAMON GUMMIES

Serves: 4

Nutritional Information (per serving):
Calories: 17 | Carbohydrates: 0g | Fats: 0g | Protein: 4g

INGREDIENTS:

- 1 cup water
- 2 tbsp natural sweetener
- 5 - 10 drops of cinnamon oil
- 1 - 2 scoops of stevia extract
- 3 tbsp agar agar
- Red food coloring

EQUIPMENT:

- Gummy mold

DIRECTIONS:

1. Mix the water, natural sweetener, and cinnamon oil into a small saucepan. Bring the mixture over low - medium heat until it turns warm.
2. Add the stevia, then try the mixture. Adjust the amount of cinnamon oil and sweetener to taste.
3. Gradually whisk in the agar agar while hot. Keep mixing until all of it has dissolved.
4. Pour the mixture into the mold.
5. Refrigerate until the candy has hardened.

WATERMELON LEMONADE GUMMY CANDY

Serves: 55

Nutritional Information (per serving):
Calories: 5 | Carbohydrates: 1g | Fats: 0.5g | Protein: 0g

INGREDIENTS:

- 2 cup watermelon juice
- 1 cup fresh lemon juice
- 1/4 cup agar agar
- 2 tbsp maple syrup

EQUIPMENT:

- Gummy mold

DIRECTIONS:

1. Using a small saucepan on medium low heat, mix the watermelon juice with the fresh lemon juice. Add the maple syrup. Whisk the mixture until it is mixed thoroughly.
2. Gradually mix in the agar agar. Continue to whisk until it has dissolved.
3. Remove the mixture from the heat and pour it into gummy molds.
4. Let the gummy mixture cool in the refrigerator for about 45 minutes.

JELLO

Serves: 16

Nutritional Information (per serving):
Calories: 22 | Carbohydrates: 5g | Fats: 1g | Protein: 1g

INGREDIENTS:

- 2 cup 100% grape juice
- 3 tbsp agar agar

EQUIPMENT:

- Baking pan

DIRECTIONS:

1. Place parchment paper on a baking pan or lightly grease with cooking spray.
2. Add the grape juice and agar agar to a small saucepan. Let the mixture boil while constantly whisking to help the agar agar dissolve. Remove the pan from the heat once all the ingredients have mixed.
3. Transfer the mixture from the saucepan to the baking pan. Let it sit in the refrigerator for 2 hours. Slice the gummy into smaller squares.

ROSÉ GUMMIES

Serves: 20

Nutritional Information (per serving):
Calories: 22 | Carbohydrates: 3g | Fats: 0g | Protein: 0g

INGREDIENTS:

- 1 cup Rosé wine
- 2 tbsp maple syrup
- 1 tbsp agar agar

EQUIPMENT:

- Gummy mold

DIRECTIONS:

1. Start by placing your mold of choice in the freezer.
2. Mix all the ingredients together in a saucepan. Continue whisking in the agar agar until it has completely mixed.
3. Bring the mixture to a simmer while continuously stirring. Do this for 3 minutes.
4. Remove the mixture from the heat and let it sit for 5 minutes.
5. Take the mold out from the freezer and pour the liquid mixture in.
6. Put it back in the freezer for another 10 minutes.
7. Remove the gummy candy from the mold.

COCONUT TURMERIC GUMMIES

Serves: 12

Nutritional Information (per serving):
Calories: 52 | Carbohydrates: 3.2g | Fats: 4.1g | Protein: 1.5g

INGREDIENTS:

- 1 cup coconut milk
- 2 tbsp fresh ginger, grated
- 2 tbsp coconut sugar
- 1 tbsp fresh turmeric, grated
- 2 tbsp agar agar

EQUIPMENT:

- Gummy mold

DIRECTIONS:

1. Combine the coconut milk, grated ginger, grated turmeric, and coconut sugar in a small saucepan. Bring the mixture to a simmer.
2. Remove the mixture from the heat. Let it sit for 15 to 30 minutes.
3. Strain the mixture into a bowl using a fine mesh strainer. With the back of a spoon, mash the ginger and turmeric into the strainer to juice them out.
4. Rinse the saucepan and put the mixture back inside.
5. Sprinkle agar agar gradually into the pan. Use a whisk to help you get rid of any chunks. Then, let the mixture sit for 3 to 5 minutes to undergo the process of blooming.
6. Set the heat back to low while thoroughly whisking the mixture. The agar agar should thoroughly melt and have a smooth consistency.

7. Remove the mixture from the heat. Transfer the mixture into the molds.
8. Refrigerate the candy for 30 minutes.
9. Remove the candy from the molds and serve.

GREEN TEA, LEMON, AND GINGER GUMMIES

Serves: 1

Nutritional Information (per serving):
Calories: 15 | Carbohydrates: 2g | Fats: 1.6g | Protein: 0g

INGREDIENTS:

- 3/4 cup cold water
- 5 tbsp agar agar flakes
- 1/2 cup strongly brewed green tea with 4 tea bags
- 6 tbsp ginger juice
- 1/4 cup lemon juice

EQUIPMENT:

- Gummy mold

DIRECTIONS:

1. In a saucepan, pour the cold water. Sprinkle in the agar agar flakes and let it dissolve. Set it aside.
2. Combine the brewed tea, ginger juice, and lemon juice with the agar agar mixture. Gently heat the pan and whisk until all agar agar has dissolved.
3. Pour the mixture into a gummy mold. Leave it in the refrigerator for at least 2 hours.

Made in the USA
Coppell, TX
27 March 2021

52465571R00037